The Financial Bullet Blueprint

Alex Thompson

Published by Side Hustle Success, 2023.

While every precaution has been taken in the preparation of this book, the publisher assumes no responsibility for errors or omissions, or for damages resulting from the use of the information contained herein.

THE FINANCIAL BULLET BLUEPRINT

First edition. July 24, 2023.

ISBN: 979-8223596240

Written by Alex Thompson.

Also by Alex Thompson

Alex on Finance

Financial Freedom Roadmap - Achieving Early Retirement through the FIRE Movement

The Art of Strategic Innovation

Beyond Cash - The Evolution of Digital Payment Systems and the Future of Money

Preserving Wealth in Inflationary Times - Strategies for Protecting Your Financial Future

Standalone

Side Hustle Success: Unlocking Your Entrepreneurial Potential

Side Hustle Success: The Ultimate Guide to Passive and Financial Freedom

Mastering the Markets: Advanced Trading Strategies for Success and Ethical Trading Practices

Financial Fortitude

Mastering the Art of Upselling

The Financial Bullet Blueprint

Table of Contents

Chapter 1: Understanding Your Financial Landscape 1

Chapter 2: Crafting Your Financial Vision 9

Chapter 3: The Budgeting Masterplan 15

Chapter 4: Saving Strategies for Financial Success 23

Chapter 5: Demystifying Investments 31

Chapter 6: Building Your Investment Portfolio 39

Chapter 7: Navigating Debt and Credit 47

Chapter 8: Realizing Financial Freedom 55

Chapter 9: Safeguarding Your Financial Future 63

Chapter 10: Mastering the Financial Mindset 71

Chapter 1: Understanding Your Financial Landscape

- Welcome to the beginning of your journey towards financial success! Just as an explorer needs to understand the lay of the land before embarking on an adventure, you must comprehend your financial landscape to achieve your dreams and aspirations. Think of this chapter as your compass, guiding you through the importance of financial literacy—a crucial tool in this exciting expedition.
- Picture yourself at the helm of your financial ship, steering towards a future of prosperity and freedom. Financial literacy acts as your compass, ensuring you stay on course and avoid drifting into uncharted waters. But what exactly is financial literacy, and why is it so significant?
- At its core, financial literacy is the knowledge and understanding of various financial concepts and practices that empower you to make informed decisions about your money. It's like having a map that reveals the hidden pathways to financial success and warns you of potential pitfalls.
- As you embark on this voyage of discovery, keep in mind the following reasons why financial literacy matters:
- **1. Empowerment and Control:** Imagine the satisfaction of being the captain of your financial ship, confidently charting its course. Financial literacy grants you that power, allowing you to take charge of your financial life. You'll be able to set sail towards your goals with the wind in your favor.
- **2. Breaking the Cycle of Debt:** In the turbulent sea of financial decisions, those lacking financial literacy can easily find themselves shipwrecked by debt. However, with a firm grasp of financial concepts, you can navigate away from

treacherous waters and avoid drowning in debts.

- **3. Building a Strong Foundation:** Like constructing a sturdy lighthouse, financial literacy creates a solid base for your financial structure. It ensures that each brick of your financial decisions is well-placed, supporting the growth of your wealth over time.
- **4. Seizing Opportunities:** Financial literacy acts as a spyglass, allowing you to spot opportunities that others might miss. From savvy investments to money-saving strategies, you'll have the tools to seize the best opportunities that come your way.
- **5. Weathering Storms:** Life's financial waters can be unpredictable, with storms of economic downturns and unexpected expenses. But equipped with financial literacy, you can navigate these challenges with confidence, safeguarding your financial ship against potential damage.
- Are you ready to take the helm and steer your financial ship towards success? Throughout this book, we will equip you with the knowledge and skills to read the stars of finance, plot your course, and reach the shores of financial independence. So hoist the sails of curiosity, and let's set forth on this exhilarating journey together!
-

Assessing Your Current Financial Situation

- As you embark on your financial journey, the first crucial step is to take stock of your current financial situation. Think of this as conducting an expedition of self-discovery, where you'll map out your financial landscape with accuracy and precision. By assessing your current position, you gain a clear understanding of where you stand financially and can chart a course towards your goals. Here's how to navigate this assessment process:
- **1. Gather All Financial Information:** Assemble all your

financial documents, including bank statements, investment account statements, credit card bills, loan statements, and any other relevant paperwork. This will form the foundation of your financial map.

- **2. Calculate Your Net Worth:** To determine your net worth, subtract your liabilities (debts) from your assets. Your assets may include savings, investments, real estate, and other valuable possessions, while liabilities consist of loans, credit card debts, and outstanding bills. This calculation reveals your current financial position.
- **3. Analyze Your Income and Expenses:** Track your income sources and analyze your monthly expenses. Categorize your spending to understand where your money is going. This process helps identify areas where you can cut back on unnecessary expenses and potentially increase your savings.
- **4. Review Debt Obligations:** Examine the types and amounts of debts you owe. Identify high-interest debts that might be weighing you down and explore strategies to manage and reduce them effectively.
- **5. Evaluate Your Credit Score:** Your credit score impacts your ability to access credit and favorable interest rates. Obtain your credit report and review it for accuracy. Address any errors and work on improving your credit score over time.
- **6. Assess Your Financial Goals:** Reflect on your short-term and long-term financial goals. Are you saving for a down payment on a house, planning for retirement, or dreaming of starting your own business? Understanding your aspirations will help you tailor your financial plan accordingly.
- **7. Consider Risk Tolerance:** Assess your comfort level with

financial risks. Are you willing to take higher risks for potentially higher returns, or do you prefer a more conservative approach? Understanding your risk tolerance is vital for crafting an investment strategy that aligns with your comfort level.

- **8. Reflect on Financial Habits:** Take a moment to evaluate your financial habits. Do you tend to save diligently or often find yourself splurging on impulse purchases? Acknowledging your habits allows you to make conscious changes for the better.
- By thoroughly assessing your current financial situation, you'll draw the map that reveals the starting point of your journey. Remember, this process is about self-discovery and honesty, setting the stage for the transformative steps that lie ahead. With this knowledge in hand, you're ready to move forward and navigate towards your financial goals with confidence.
-

Identifying Your Financial Goals and Aspirations

- Just like an explorer sets their sights on distant horizons, you must define your financial goals and aspirations to navigate towards a brighter financial future. These goals act as the guiding stars that will keep you on course throughout your journey. Let's embark on the process of identifying your financial goals and aspirations:
- **1. Short-Term vs. Long-Term Goals:** Begin by distinguishing between short-term and long-term financial goals. Short-term goals might include building an emergency fund, paying off credit card debt, or saving for a vacation. Long-term goals, on the other hand, encompass major milestones like purchasing a home, funding your children's education, or achieving financial independence in retirement.

- **2. Make Your Goals Specific:** Clearly articulate each goal in specific terms. Instead of saying, "I want to save more money," specify the exact amount you aim to save, like "I want to save $10,000 for a down payment on a house."
- **3. Set Measurable Milestones:** Break down your larger financial goals into smaller, measurable milestones. These milestones act as markers of progress and provide a sense of accomplishment as you reach each one.
- **4. Align Goals with Values:** Consider your core values when setting financial goals. Aligning your financial pursuits with your values ensures that your decisions feel purposeful and fulfilling.
- **5. Prioritize Your Goals:** You may have multiple financial aspirations, but it's essential to prioritize them based on urgency and significance. Determine which goals are most critical to tackle first and allocate resources accordingly.
- **6. Establish a Timeframe:** Set realistic timelines for achieving your financial goals. A specific timeframe adds a sense of urgency and keeps you focused on taking action.
- **7. Visualize Your Goals:** Create a visual representation of your financial goals. Whether it's a vision board, a written description, or an image that symbolizes your aspirations, visualizing your goals strengthens your commitment and keeps them at the forefront of your mind.
- **8. Consider Financial Freedom:** Reflect on what financial freedom means to you. Is it retiring comfortably, pursuing your passions without financial constraints, or achieving a specific level of income? Understanding your definition of financial freedom shapes your entire financial journey.

- **9. Review and Revise:** As you progress on your financial journey, be open to reviewing and revising your goals. Life circumstances and priorities may change, and it's essential to adapt your goals accordingly.
- **10. Make Goals Challenging Yet Attainable:** Set ambitious financial goals that push you to grow and achieve more, but ensure they remain realistic and achievable. Overly lofty goals can lead to frustration, while easily attainable goals might not challenge you to reach your full potential.
- Identifying your financial goals and aspirations is a pivotal step in your financial blueprint. Each goal you define becomes a compass point guiding you in the right direction. So, dream big, envision the life you desire, and let your financial aspirations propel you forward on this extraordinary voyage to wealth and financial independence.
- **Exploring the Psychology of Money and Its Impact on Decision-Making**
- Ah, the fascinating realm of the mind—the hidden currents that influence our financial choices and steer the course of our financial journey. Understanding the psychology of money is like unraveling the mysteries of the deep sea—a captivating and enlightening expedition. Let's dive into the intricacies of how our thoughts, emotions, and beliefs about money influence our decision-making:
- **1. Unearthing Money Beliefs:** Our relationship with money often stems from deep-rooted beliefs and experiences formed during childhood. Explore your money beliefs, whether they're based on abundance, scarcity, or something in between. Recognizing these beliefs will enable you to better comprehend your financial behaviors.
- **2. Emotional Influences on Money Decisions:** Emotions and

financial decisions are closely intertwined. Fear, greed, anxiety, and euphoria can all impact the choices we make with money. Awareness of these emotional triggers allows us to pause, assess, and make more rational decisions.

- **3. Cognitive Biases and Financial Mistakes:** As explorers navigating uncharted waters, we must be aware of cognitive biases that cloud our judgment. Common biases, such as confirmation bias (favoring information that confirms our existing beliefs) or loss aversion (fearing losses more than appreciating gains), can lead to costly financial mistakes.
- **4. The Role of Impulse and Delayed Gratification:** Instant gratification might offer a fleeting thrill, but it can undermine our long-term financial goals. Discover the power of delayed gratification, the art of patiently waiting for larger rewards and making wise financial choices for the future.
- **5. The Impact of Social Influence:** Just as the tides are influenced by the moon, our financial decisions can be swayed by societal pressures and norms. Peer pressure, marketing tactics, and societal expectations often impact how we spend and save our money.
- **6. Creating Positive Financial Habits:** Just like skilled sailors, we can learn to navigate the waters of money by developing positive financial habits. Cultivate habits like budgeting, regular saving, and automating finances to ensure your financial ship stays on course.
- **7. Overcoming Money Mindset Barriers:** The storms of negative money mindsets can hinder our progress. Learn how to overcome limiting beliefs about money and cultivate a growth mindset that encourages financial learning and

improvement.

- **8. Seeking Professional Guidance:** Sometimes, even experienced explorers seek the guidance of seasoned navigators. Similarly, seeking help from financial advisors or coaches can provide valuable insights and keep you on track to achieve your financial goals.
- **9. Emotional Intelligence and Financial Success:** Emotions are an integral part of our lives, and developing emotional intelligence can profoundly impact our financial well-being. Learn to understand and manage emotions in the context of money to make more informed decisions.
- **10. Building Resilience:** Like ships that brave storms and stay afloat, financial resilience allows us to weather life's uncertainties. Strengthen your financial resilience by preparing for emergencies, building diversified portfolios, and having contingency plans in place.
- Understanding the psychology of money is like having a compass that reveals the hidden currents guiding our financial decisions. As you delve into this captivating realm, you'll gain valuable insights that will empower you to steer your financial ship with greater wisdom and self-awareness. So, hoist the sail of curiosity, and let the exploration of money psychology begin!

Chapter 2: Crafting Your Financial Vision

- **Defining Your Long-Term Financial Objectives**
- Welcome to the heart of your financial journey—a chapter that sets the course for your aspirations and dreams. Like a master shipbuilder creating a grand vessel, you will craft your financial vision with precision and purpose. Let's set our compass on the horizon and chart the course:
- **1. Envision Your Ideal Financial Future:** Close your eyes and imagine your ideal financial future. What does it look like? Visualize where you want to be in five, ten, or twenty years from now. Consider every aspect, from your career and lifestyle to your family and community.
- **2. Align Your Financial Goals with Your Vision:** Your financial goals are the building blocks of your vision. Ensure that each goal you set aligns with your broader financial vision. Picture each goal as a vital part of the grand ship you're constructing to sail towards your dream life.
- **3. Reflect on Your Passions and Interests:** As you shape your financial vision, consider your passions and interests. How can your financial choices support and enrich the things that truly matter to you? By integrating your passions, you'll create a more fulfilling and purpose-driven journey.
- **4. Set Specific Milestones for Your Vision:** Just as explorers mark the waypoints on their maps, establish specific milestones along your financial journey. These milestones serve as checkpoints, guiding your progress and celebrating your achievements.
- **5. Embrace Flexibility and Adaptability:** The seas of life can be unpredictable, and your financial journey may encounter

storms and unexpected currents. Embrace flexibility in your financial vision, allowing you to adapt your course while keeping your ultimate destination in sight.

- **6. Incorporate Financial Independence and Retirement:** Financial independence and retirement are often significant milestones in the voyage of life. Factor these into your financial vision, imagining a future where you have the freedom to pursue your passions without financial constraints.
- **7. Balance the Present and the Future:** As you define your long-term financial objectives, strike a balance between enjoying the present and planning for the future. Cherish the experiences of today while investing in a secure and prosperous tomorrow.
- **8. Seek Inspiration and Role Models:** Just as sailors draw inspiration from legendary explorers, seek inspiration from financial role models who have achieved similar goals. Learn from their successes and challenges, applying their wisdom to your own journey.
- **9. Communicate Your Vision:** Sharing your financial vision with trusted loved ones can strengthen your commitment and create a support network. When those around you understand and share your aspirations, they can offer encouragement and understanding along the way.
- **10. Revise and Refine Your Vision Periodically:** Your financial vision is not carved in stone. As your life evolves, so might your aspirations. Periodically review, revise, and refine your financial vision to ensure it remains authentic and relevant to your changing circumstances.
- Crafting your financial vision is like hoisting the sails of purpose, propelling you towards the life you envision. As you

set your eyes on the distant horizons of your dreams, the map you've drawn will guide you through every twist and turn of your financial voyage. So, set your compass on the stars of possibility, and let the journey towards your financial vision begin!

- **Setting SMART (Specific, Measurable, Achievable, Relevant, Time-bound) Financial Goals**
- Just as skilled navigators meticulously plot their course using precise coordinates, you will set sail towards your financial vision with SMART financial goals. These beacons of direction will guide you towards success, ensuring that your efforts are focused, measurable, and attainable. Let's explore the power of SMART financial goals and how they chart the course to your dreams:
- **1. Specific Goals:** Specificity is the compass that provides clear direction. Instead of vague aspirations like "I want to be wealthy," define your financial goals with clarity. For example, "I will save $10,000 for a down payment on a house within two years."
- **2. Measurable Milestones:** Just like sailors measure their progress using nautical miles, you'll break down your financial goals into measurable milestones. These milestones allow you to track your progress and celebrate achievements along the way.
- **3. Achievable Objectives:** While dreaming big is encouraged, setting unrealistic financial goals can lead to frustration and burnout. Ensure your goals are achievable based on your current financial situation and resources.
- **4. Relevant to Your Vision:** Ensure that each financial goal you set aligns with your broader financial vision. Each goal

should serve a purpose, contributing to the realization of your dream life.

- **5. Time-Bound Targets:** Just as explorers set sail with a clear timeline in mind, attach deadlines to your financial goals. A defined timeframe creates a sense of urgency and encourages consistent action.
- **Example of a SMART Financial Goal:**
- **Non-SMART Goal:** "I want to invest in the stock market."
- **SMART Goal:** "I will invest $5,000 in a diversified portfolio of stocks and bonds within the next six months to build wealth for my long-term financial independence."
- Setting SMART financial goals ensures that your financial ship stays on course, navigating through the vast ocean of possibilities with precision and purpose. Each goal you set becomes a guiding star, leading you towards the realization of your financial vision. So, unfurl the sails of determination, and let the power of SMART goals propel you towards the life you desire.

Creating a Vision Board or Financial Vision Statement

As explorers map their expeditions with detailed charts, you will craft a visual representation of your financial dreams through a vision board or financial vision statement. These tools act as your compass, keeping your financial vision alive and inspiring you to stay the course. Let's dive into the creative process of crafting your financial vision:

1. Vision Board:

- Gather Materials: Start by collecting magazines, newspapers, photographs, and any other materials that resonate with your financial aspirations.
- Visual Representation: Use these materials to create a collage

of images and words that represent your financial goals and dreams. Include pictures of your dream home, the destinations you want to travel to, or any other financial achievements you desire.

- Display with Purpose: Place your vision board in a prominent location where you'll see it daily—your bedroom, office, or even as your phone's wallpaper. Each glance will reinforce your vision and remind you of your destination.

2. Financial Vision Statement:

- Reflect on Your Vision: Take time to reflect on your long-term financial objectives and the life you envision.
- Write from the Heart: Compose a clear and concise statement that captures the essence of your financial vision. Use powerful language and descriptive terms to paint a vivid picture of your future.
- Include Specific Goals: Incorporate specific financial goals and milestones within your vision statement.
- Review and Refine: Review your financial vision statement regularly, refining it as your aspirations evolve.

Example of a Financial Vision Statement:

"I am financially independent, living a life of purpose and abundance. I own a beautiful home by the sea, and my investment portfolio generates passive income that allows me to pursue my passions and travel the world. I am debt-free and have a secure retirement plan in place. My financial choices align with my values, and I am committed to giving back to my community and making a positive impact on the lives of others. Every day, I take steps towards achieving my financial dreams and enjoying the freedom and fulfillment that comes with financial success."

Both vision boards and financial vision statements serve as powerful tools to keep your financial vision alive and focused. They remind you of the life you are striving to create, providing motivation and inspiration during challenging times. So, set your imagination free, and let the creativity of your financial vision take shape—your compass towards an extraordinary financial journey.

Chapter 3: The Budgeting Masterplan

Creating a Personalized Budget that Aligns with Your Financial Goals

In the financial journey you've embarked upon, the budget is the captain's wheel that steers your ship towards financial success. Just as skilled navigators chart their course with precision, you will craft a personalized budget that aligns with your unique financial goals. Now, we will set sail on the budgeting masterplan, a strategic framework to guide you through the art of budgeting:

1. Understand the Purpose of Budgeting:

- Budgeting is not about restriction; it's about financial empowerment. It allows you to take control of your money, directing it towards your goals with purpose and intention.

2. Track Your Income and Expenses:

- Begin by diligently tracking your income from all sources, including salaries, bonuses, investments, and side hustles. Similarly, record your expenses, both fixed (rent, utilities) and variable (entertainment, dining out).

3. Categorize Your Spending:

- Categorize your expenses into essential and discretionary categories. This classification will help you identify areas where you can potentially reduce expenses and allocate more funds towards your financial goals.

4. Determine Your Financial Goals:

- Refer back to the financial vision you crafted and identify the specific financial goals you want to achieve. Whether it's saving for a down payment, paying off debt, or building an emergency fund, each goal will guide your budgeting efforts.

5. Allocate Funds to Your Goals:

- Allocate a portion of your income to each financial goal. Prioritize your goals based on their urgency and significance, ensuring that they receive the attention they deserve within your budget.

6. Create a Realistic Budget:

- Be honest with yourself and create a budget that aligns with your current financial situation. Avoid overestimating your income or underestimating your expenses, as this may lead to frustration and challenges in sticking to the budget.

7. Account for Irregular Expenses:

- Remember to factor in irregular expenses, such as annual insurance premiums or holiday gifts, in your budget. Set aside a portion of your income each month for these infrequent but expected costs.

8. Embrace Technology and Apps:

- Utilize budgeting apps and financial tools to simplify the budgeting process. These digital companions can help you track your spending, categorize expenses, and provide valuable insights into your financial habits.

9. Monitor and Adjust:

- Your budget is not static; it's a living document that should be monitored and adjusted regularly. Review your budget periodically to ensure you stay on track and make adjustments as needed.

10. Celebrate Progress:

- Celebrate your budgeting victories, no matter how small. Each step towards your financial goals is an achievement worth acknowledging.

Crafting a personalized budget is the compass that guides your financial voyage. With each carefully considered allocation of funds, you will navigate towards your goals with confidence and determination. So, hoist the sails of financial planning, and let the budgeting masterplan set the course for your financial success.

Tracking Expenses and Identifying Areas for Improvement

As skilled navigators meticulously chart their course, you will navigate your financial journey by tracking expenses—a vital practice to maintain control over your financial ship. By logging your expenditures, you'll gain valuable insights into your spending habits and identify areas where you can improve. Let's delve into the process of tracking expenses and optimizing your financial route:

1. Choose a Tracking Method:

- Select a tracking method that suits your lifestyle and preferences. You can use traditional pen-and-paper methods, spreadsheets, or opt for modern budgeting apps that automatically categorize your expenses.

2. Record Daily Transactions:

- Make it a habit to record every expense, no matter how small, on a daily basis. This comprehensive approach ensures accuracy in your budgeting analysis.

3. Categorize Your Expenses:

- Organize your expenses into categories to understand where your money is going. Common categories include housing, transportation, food, entertainment, and utilities.

4. Analyze Spending Patterns:

- Regularly review your expense log to identify spending patterns and trends. Are there areas where you consistently overspend? Are there discretionary expenses that could be reduced to allocate more funds to your financial goals?

5. Differentiate Wants vs. Needs:

- Distinguish between essential expenses (needs) and non-essential discretionary spending (wants). Prioritize your needs while being mindful of your wants to maintain a balanced budget.

6. Identify Areas for Reduction:

- Pinpoint categories where you can cut back on spending. Look for opportunities to save, such as negotiating bills, finding more cost-effective alternatives, or eliminating unnecessary subscriptions.

7. Set Realistic Spending Targets:

- Use your expense analysis to set realistic spending targets for each category. These targets will guide your day-to-day spending and keep you on track with your budget.

8. Adopt Frugal Habits:

- Embrace frugality as you make intentional choices to save money. Small adjustments, like preparing meals at home or exploring free entertainment options, can add up to significant savings over time.

9. Track Progress and Celebrate Success:

- Regularly monitor your progress in adhering to your budget and achieving your financial goals. Celebrate milestones and achievements, reinforcing positive financial habits.

10. Stay Committed to Improvement:

- Tracking expenses is an ongoing process, and staying committed to improvement is essential. Learn from your spending patterns and continue to optimize your budget as your financial situation evolves.

By tracking expenses and identifying areas for improvement, you gain a deeper understanding of your financial choices. This awareness empowers you to make informed decisions, adjust your course as needed, and stay on track towards your financial destination. So, set sail on the voyage of expense tracking, and let your financial insights navigate you to prosperity.

Tips for Staying Disciplined with Your Budget

As expert sailors stay disciplined with their navigation, you too can maintain financial discipline and stay on course with your budget. Staying committed to your budget is vital for achieving your financial goals and ensuring a smooth journey to financial success. Here are some valuable tips to help you remain steadfast in your financial discipline:

1. Set Clear Financial Goals:

- A clear vision of your financial goals provides motivation and purpose for sticking to your budget. Remind yourself of the rewards that await you as you stay disciplined and make progress towards your aspirations.

2. Establish a Realistic Budget:

- Craft a budget that aligns with your current financial situation and lifestyle. A realistic budget is easier to follow and less likely to cause feelings of deprivation.

3. Make Your Budget Visible:

- Keep your budget in plain sight, whether as a printed document on your fridge or a digital budgeting app on your phone. Regularly seeing your budget reinforces your commitment to its guidelines.

4. Automate Savings and Bill Payments:

- Set up automatic transfers to your savings and investment accounts as soon as you receive your income. Automating bill payments ensures you never miss due dates and incur unnecessary fees.

5. Use Cash or Envelope Systems:

- For discretionary spending categories like groceries or entertainment, consider using cash or envelope systems. This method provides a tangible limit, making it easier to control expenses in those areas.

6. Practice Mindful Spending:

- Pause before making any non-essential purchase and ask yourself if it aligns with your financial goals. Practicing mindful spending helps curb impulse purchases and stay focused on your priorities.

7. Reward Yourself Occasionally:

- Building discipline doesn't mean depriving yourself entirely. Include occasional rewards within your budget to celebrate milestones or accomplishments—just be sure they fit within your financial plan.

8. Seek Support and Accountability:

- Share your budgeting journey with a trusted friend or family member who can provide encouragement and hold you accountable. Discussing your progress with someone you trust strengthens your commitment.

9. Review and Revise Regularly:

- Review your budget regularly to assess your progress and identify any areas that need adjustment. Life circumstances may change, and your budget should adapt accordingly.

10. Stay Positive and Patient:

- Financial discipline takes time and practice. Be patient with yourself, and stay positive even if you face occasional setbacks. Focus on the progress you've made and keep moving forward.

Staying disciplined with your budget is like steering your financial ship through calm and turbulent waters with determination and skill. As you build discipline, you'll gain greater control over your financial journey, guiding your ship towards your desired destination of financial success. So, embrace the strength of discipline, and let it be the wind that propels you forward on this extraordinary voyage to prosperity.

Chapter 4: Saving Strategies for Financial Success

The Power of Compound Interest and Time in Building Wealth

Welcome to the treasure trove of financial success—a chapter that reveals the secrets of building wealth through the potent combination of compound interest and time. Just as patient explorers unearth hidden treasures, you will discover how these two forces work together to grow your wealth exponentially. Let's embark on this enlightening journey to understand the magic behind compound interest and time:

1. Understanding Compound Interest:

- Compound interest is the eighth wonder of the world, as famously quoted by Albert Einstein. It refers to the interest earned not only on the initial principal but also on the accumulated interest from previous periods. Over time, this compounding effect accelerates your wealth growth.

2. Embrace the Power of Time:

- Time is the most valuable asset when it comes to building wealth. The earlier you start saving and investing, the longer your money has to grow through the wonders of compound interest.

3. Start Saving Early:

- Begin saving and investing as early as possible, even if it's with small amounts. The power of compounding allows your money to work for you and significantly amplify your wealth over time.

4. Be Consistent with Savings:

- Consistency is key to maximizing the benefits of compound interest. Regularly contribute to your savings and investment accounts, making it a habit to add to your wealth-building efforts.

5. Maximize Retirement Contributions:

- Take advantage of tax-advantaged retirement accounts, such as 401(k)s and IRAs. These accounts allow your investments to grow tax-free or tax-deferred, boosting your wealth-building potential.

6. Diversify Your Investments:

- Diversification spreads your investments across various asset classes, reducing risk and enhancing long-term returns. A well-diversified portfolio benefits from the cumulative effects of compound interest.

7. Reinvest Dividends and Interest:

- Reinvesting dividends and interest earned from your investments allows your money to compound faster. Instead of withdrawing these earnings, let them reinvest and grow over time.

8. Avoid High-Interest Debt:

- Compound interest can work against you when it comes to high-interest debt. Minimize or eliminate debts with high interest rates to free up more of your income for savings and investments.

9. Stay Committed to Long-Term Goals:

- Building wealth through compound interest requires patience and a long-term perspective. Stay committed to your financial goals, trusting the power of time to work in your favor.

10. Educate Yourself on Investing:

- As explorers study maps and navigation, educate yourself about investing and personal finance. Knowledge empowers you to make informed decisions and capitalize on wealth-building opportunities.

The power of compound interest and time is the wind beneath the wings of your financial journey. With each passing year, the magic of compounding multiplies your wealth, making the seemingly impossible dreams within reach. So, set sail with the power of compound interest, and let time be your ally on this exciting voyage to financial abundance and success.

Differentiating Between Short-Term and Long-Term Savings Goals

In the vast ocean of financial planning, distinguishing between short-term and long-term savings goals is like charting different courses for distinct destinations. Each type of goal requires its own approach and strategies. Let's navigate through the differences between these two types of savings goals:

1. Short-Term Savings Goals:

- Short-term savings goals are those you aim to achieve within a relatively brief period, typically within one year or less.

- Examples of short-term goals include creating an emergency fund, saving for a vacation, buying a new gadget, or paying off a small debt.
- These goals often have a specific target amount and a defined timeframe for completion.

2. Strategies for Short-Term Goals:

- Prioritize liquidity and accessibility for short-term savings. Consider using a high-yield savings account or a money market account for easy access to your funds.
- Focus on consistency and regular contributions to meet the short timeframe for achieving these goals.
- Budget carefully and allocate funds specifically for short-term savings to avoid tapping into long-term investments or incurring high-interest debt.

3. Long-Term Savings Goals:

- Long-term savings goals are those you plan to achieve over an extended period, often several years or decades into the future.
- Examples of long-term goals include saving for retirement, buying a home, funding your children's education, or building significant wealth for financial independence.
- Long-term goals typically require substantial contributions over time due to their magnitude and extended timeframe.

4. Strategies for Long-Term Goals:

- Emphasize growth potential and consider long-term investments, such as stocks and bonds, to benefit from compounding and potential higher returns.
- Take advantage of tax-advantaged retirement accounts like IRAs and 401(k)s to maximize tax benefits and accumulate

more funds over time.

- Reassess and adjust your long-term savings strategies periodically to align with changes in your financial situation and market conditions.

5. Balancing Short-Term and Long-Term Goals:

- Achieving financial success involves striking a balance between short-term and long-term goals. While focusing on immediate needs, it's essential not to neglect the importance of long-term financial security and growth.
- Prioritize emergency savings first, as it provides a safety net and allows you to face unexpected expenses without derailing your long-term plans.

6. Review and Reevaluate:

- Regularly review your short-term and long-term goals, assessing your progress and making adjustments as necessary. Life circumstances and priorities may change, and your savings strategies should adapt accordingly.

By differentiating between short-term and long-term savings goals, you can steer your financial ship towards multiple destinations—both immediate and distant. Each type of goal requires a unique approach, but together, they form a comprehensive financial plan that leads to a prosperous and fulfilling journey. So, navigate with purpose, and let your savings strategies guide you towards financial success on this extraordinary voyage.

Strategies for Automating Savings and Managing Emergency Funds

As skilled navigators streamline their routes with efficient systems, you too can optimize your financial journey by automating savings and establishing a robust emergency fund. Let's explore these strategies to ensure a smoother sail towards financial security:

1. Automating Savings:

- Set up automatic transfers from your checking account to your savings or investment accounts. By automating your savings, you ensure that a portion of your income is consistently directed towards your financial goals without requiring manual effort.

2. Pay Yourself First:

- Treat your savings as a non-negotiable expense, just like paying bills. Prioritize saving a portion of your income before allocating funds to discretionary spending.

3. Utilize Direct Deposit:

- If possible, arrange for your employer to deposit a portion of your salary directly into your savings account. This strategy eliminates the temptation to spend the money before saving it.

4. Establish Multiple Savings Buckets:

- Create separate savings accounts for different goals. For example, have one account for emergencies, another for vacation savings, and a third for long-term investments. This organization helps you track progress towards each goal more effectively.

5. Emergency Fund Essentials:

- Aim to build an emergency fund that covers three to six

months' worth of living expenses. This fund provides a safety net during unexpected financial setbacks, such as job loss or medical emergencies.

6. Set Clear Emergency Fund Rules:

- Determine the criteria for using your emergency fund. For example, it should only be tapped into for genuine emergencies, not for impulsive purchases or non-essential expenses.

7. Replenish Your Emergency Fund:

- If you use your emergency fund, prioritize replenishing it as soon as possible. This ensures that it remains available for future unforeseen circumstances.

8. Use High-Yield Savings Accounts:

- Keep your emergency fund and short-term savings in high-yield savings accounts. These accounts offer better interest rates than regular savings accounts, helping your funds grow over time.

9. Regularly Reevaluate Savings Goals:

- Review your financial goals periodically and adjust your automated savings contributions accordingly. Life circumstances and priorities may change, and your savings strategy should adapt accordingly.

10. Monitor Account Activity:

- Regularly check your savings and emergency fund accounts to ensure that automated transfers are functioning correctly. Also, review your progress towards savings goals and make adjustments as needed.

By automating savings and managing your emergency fund, you set your financial ship on autopilot, ensuring that you stay on course towards financial security and prosperity. These strategies not only simplify your financial journey but also provide peace of mind, knowing that your savings are growing steadily and that you have a safety net in times of need. So, hoist the sails of automation, and let the wind of financial stability guide you on this remarkable voyage to a brighter future.

Chapter 5: Demystifying Investments

An Overview of Different Investment Vehicles (Stocks, Bonds, Mutual Funds, Real Estate, etc.)

In the vast ocean of financial opportunities, navigating the world of investments can seem daunting. However, fear not, for in this chapter, we will demystify various investment vehicles and help you understand their potential benefits and risks. Like seasoned navigators exploring diverse territories, you will gain an overview of these investments and make informed decisions for your financial journey:

1. Stocks:

- Stocks represent ownership in a company. When you buy shares of a company's stock, you become a partial owner, entitled to potential profits through price appreciation and dividends. Stocks offer growth potential, but their values can be volatile.

2. Bonds:

- Bonds are debt securities where investors lend money to governments or corporations in exchange for regular interest payments (coupon) and the return of the principal amount at maturity. Bonds are generally considered lower-risk investments than stocks.

3. Mutual Funds:

- Mutual funds pool money from multiple investors to invest in a diversified portfolio of stocks, bonds, or other assets. They are managed by professional fund managers and offer instant diversification for investors.

4. Exchange-Traded Funds (ETFs):

- ETFs are similar to mutual funds, but they trade on stock exchanges like individual stocks. They offer diversification and flexibility, and their prices fluctuate throughout the trading day.

5. Real Estate Investment Trusts (REITs):

- REITs are companies that own, operate, or finance income-generating real estate. Investors can buy shares of REITs, providing exposure to the real estate market without directly owning properties.

6. Certificates of Deposit (CDs):

- CDs are time-bound deposits offered by banks with fixed interest rates and maturity dates. They are low-risk investments but typically offer lower returns than other options.

7. Commodities:

- Commodities include physical goods like gold, silver, oil, or agricultural products. Investors can gain exposure to commodity prices through various investment instruments.

8. Retirement Accounts:

- Retirement accounts, such as IRAs and 401(k)s, offer tax advantages to encourage long-term savings for retirement. They often include a range of investment options to suit individual risk tolerances.

9. Annuities:

- Annuities are insurance contracts that offer periodic payments over a set period or for the rest of an individual's life. They provide a source of income, particularly for retirees, but may come with fees and complex terms.

10. Risk and Diversification:

- Understanding the risk associated with different investments is crucial. Diversifying your portfolio by investing in a variety of assets can help manage risk and optimize returns.

As you navigate the realm of investments, remember to conduct thorough research, consider your risk tolerance, and align your choices with your financial goals. Each investment vehicle presents unique opportunities and challenges, much like uncharted territories that explorers encounter. With careful consideration and knowledge, you can harness the power of investments to propel your financial ship towards a prosperous and secure future. So, set sail with confidence, and let your investments be the guiding stars on this extraordinary voyage of wealth-building.

Risk Tolerance Assessment and Understanding Risk-Reward Dynamics

Just as skilled navigators assess the risks and rewards of uncharted waters, you too must understand your risk tolerance and the dynamics between risk and reward when it comes to investments. We'll delve into the process of assessing your risk tolerance and making informed decisions about balancing risk and reward in your investment journey:

1. Assessing Your Risk Tolerance:

- Evaluate your financial situation, investment goals, and personal temperament to determine your risk tolerance. Consider how comfortable you are with the possibility of losing money in pursuit of higher returns.

2. Time Horizon Matters:

- Your investment time horizon—how long you plan to hold your investments—plays a significant role in your risk tolerance. Longer time horizons may allow for more aggressive strategies, while shorter timeframes may necessitate a more conservative approach.

3. Risk Tolerance Questionnaire:

- Many financial institutions provide risk tolerance questionnaires to help investors gauge their risk appetite. Answering these questions honestly can provide insights into your comfort level with different types of investments.

4. Diversification and Risk Mitigation:

- Diversifying your investment portfolio across various asset classes and industries can help mitigate risk. A diversified portfolio can provide smoother returns and reduce exposure to the volatility of individual investments.

5. Understanding Risk-Return Tradeoff:

- The risk-return tradeoff refers to the idea that higher potential returns are generally associated with higher levels of risk. Investments with greater potential for growth often come with increased volatility.

6. Balancing Risk and Reward:

- Striking the right balance between risk and reward is essential. Assess your investment goals and risk tolerance to build a portfolio that aligns with your objectives and provides an acceptable level of risk.

7. Consider Long-Term Objectives:

- Long-term investment goals may afford you the opportunity to take on more risk, as the potential for recovery from short-term market fluctuations increases over time.

8. Staying Informed:

- Stay informed about economic conditions, market trends, and the performance of your investments. Knowledge empowers you to make well-informed decisions and adjust your portfolio as needed.

9. Avoid Emotional Decisions:

- Emotional reactions to market fluctuations can lead to impulsive decisions. Maintain a long-term perspective and avoid making significant changes to your portfolio based on short-term market movements.

10. Reevaluate Periodically:

- As life circumstances change, revisit your risk tolerance and investment strategy. What was suitable for you a few years ago may not be appropriate now.

By understanding your risk tolerance and the dynamics of risk and reward, you can navigate the investment landscape with greater confidence. Like a seasoned navigator, you'll make informed decisions that align with your financial goals and risk comfort level. So, set your course with prudence, and let your risk-awareness guide you towards a prosperous and rewarding investment voyage.

Diversification and Its Role in a Well-Rounded Investment Portfolio

Just as skilled navigators distribute their resources across various supplies for a successful voyage, you too can harness the power of diversification in building a well-rounded investment portfolio. Let us explore the significance of diversification and how it can help you navigate the unpredictable waters of the financial markets:

1. Understanding Diversification:

- Diversification involves spreading your investments across different asset classes, industries, and geographic regions. The goal is to reduce risk by not putting all your eggs in one basket.

2. Reducing Risk:

- Diversification is one of the most effective ways to manage risk in your investment portfolio. By holding a variety of assets, you can offset losses in one area with gains in another.

3. Asset Classes in Diversification:

- Diversify across major asset classes, such as stocks, bonds, real estate, cash, and commodities. Each asset class performs differently under various economic conditions, providing stability to your portfolio.

4. Geographic Diversification:

- Consider investing in international markets to reduce exposure to the risks associated with any single country's economy. Global diversification can protect your investments from localized risks.

5. Sector and Industry Diversification:

- Allocate your investments across different sectors and industries to avoid overconcentration in any one area. Different sectors may perform well at different stages of the economic cycle.

6. Benefits During Market Turbulence:

- Diversification can help your portfolio weather market downturns. While some investments may experience losses, others may remain stable or even gain value.

7. Risk-Return Balance:

- Diversification allows you to balance risk and potential return. Higher-risk assets may offer higher growth potential, while lower-risk assets can provide stability.

8. Long-Term Perspective:

- Diversification is most effective when viewed from a long-term perspective. While individual investments may experience short-term fluctuations, the overall portfolio can benefit from steady growth over time.

9. Rebalancing:

- Regularly rebalance your portfolio to maintain the desired asset allocation. As certain investments outperform others, rebalancing ensures that your portfolio stays in line with your risk tolerance and goals.

10. Professional Advice:

- Consider seeking advice from a financial advisor or investment professional to help you design a well-diversified portfolio tailored to your specific needs and risk profile.

By incorporating diversification into your investment strategy, you can navigate the ever-changing financial landscape with greater confidence. Like a master navigator mapping different routes, you'll construct a well-rounded investment portfolio that can withstand various market conditions and steer you towards financial success. So, set sail with diversification as your compass, and let your portfolio be a testament to the power of strategic allocation on this remarkable investment voyage.

Chapter 6: Building Your Investment Portfolio

How to Research and Select Investments That Align with Your Financial Objectives

Here we will embark on a journey of research and discovery, exploring the process of building an investment portfolio that aligns perfectly with your financial objectives. Just as expert navigators choose the best vessels for their voyage, you will learn how to select investments that fit your unique needs and goals:

1. Define Your Financial Objectives:

- Begin by clearly defining your financial objectives. Are you saving for retirement, a down payment on a house, or your children's education? Understanding your goals will shape your investment strategy.

2. Assess Your Risk Tolerance:

- Evaluate your risk tolerance to determine how comfortable you are with different levels of risk. This assessment will help you identify suitable investment options that match your risk appetite.

3. Research Different Investment Options:

- Conduct thorough research on various investment vehicles, including stocks, bonds, mutual funds, ETFs, real estate, and others. Understand their risk profiles, historical performance, and potential for growth.

4. Consider Asset Allocation:

- Decide on an asset allocation strategy that aligns with your risk tolerance and financial goals. Allocate your investments across different asset classes based on their historical returns and correlations.

5. Analyze Fundamentals:

- When investing in individual stocks or bonds, analyze the fundamentals of the companies or entities involved. Look at factors like revenue, earnings, debt levels, and management performance.

6. Utilize Financial Ratios:

- Use financial ratios such as price-to-earnings (P/E), price-to-book (P/B), and dividend yield to assess the valuation of potential investments. These ratios provide insights into the attractiveness of stocks.

7. Review Investment Costs:

- Consider the costs associated with each investment option, including management fees, expense ratios, and transaction costs. Lower-cost investments can improve your overall returns.

8. Diversification Strategy:

- Implement a diversification strategy that spreads your investments across different asset classes and industries. Diversification helps reduce risk and enhance long-term returns.

9. Seek Professional Advice (if needed):

- If you feel overwhelmed or uncertain about building your investment portfolio, consider consulting with a financial advisor. An advisor can provide personalized guidance based on your specific situation.

10. Monitor and Rebalance:

- Regularly monitor your portfolio's performance and make adjustments as needed to maintain your desired asset allocation. Rebalancing ensures that your portfolio stays in line with your goals.

Building your investment portfolio is akin to crafting a sturdy ship for your financial voyage. Each investment decision you make contributes to the strength and resilience of your portfolio. As you navigate the world of investments, remember that research and knowledge are your navigational tools, guiding you towards a successful and prosperous journey. So, set sail with confidence, and let your well-crafted investment portfolio lead you towards your financial aspirations on this extraordinary voyage of wealth-building.

Asset Allocation Strategies Based on Age, Risk Tolerance, and Financial Goals

Just as seasoned navigators adjust their course based on the winds and tides, you too can tailor your asset allocation strategy to suit your age, risk tolerance, and financial objectives. We'll explore various asset allocation approaches to help you chart the optimal course for your investment portfolio:

1. Young Investors (Aggressive Approach):

- Younger investors with a long investment horizon can typically afford to take on more risk. An aggressive approach involves allocating a higher percentage of the portfolio to growth assets like stocks, which have the potential for higher returns over the long term.

2. Middle-Aged Investors (Balanced Approach):

- Middle-aged investors may have a mix of growth and income-focused financial goals. A balanced approach involves a diversified allocation between stocks and bonds, seeking both growth and stability.

3. Pre-Retirees (Conservative Approach):

- As retirement approaches, pre-retirees often prioritize capital preservation and income generation. A conservative approach involves reducing exposure to stocks and increasing allocation to bonds and other income-generating assets.

4. Risk Tolerance-Based Approach:

- Some investors may have a higher risk tolerance and prefer a more aggressive allocation even if they are closer to retirement age. Others may be more risk-averse and opt for a conservative allocation despite being younger.

5. Goal-Based Asset Allocation:

- Tailor your asset allocation based on specific financial goals. For instance, if saving for a down payment on a house in the next five years, opt for a conservative allocation to protect the funds' principal value.

6. Time-Based Rebalancing:

- Implement a time-based rebalancing strategy to ensure that your asset allocation remains aligned with your goals. Regularly review and adjust your portfolio as your age and financial situation change.

7. Dynamic Asset Allocation:

- Employ a dynamic asset allocation approach that adjusts based on market conditions and economic outlook. This strategy allows for a more proactive response to changing investment landscapes.

8. Use Target-Date Funds (TDFs):

- Target-date funds are pre-packaged investment funds designed for specific retirement dates. They automatically adjust asset allocation over time, becoming more conservative as the target date approaches.

9. Asset Allocation Tools:

- Utilize online tools and resources to help you determine an appropriate asset allocation based on your age, risk tolerance, and financial goals. These tools can provide valuable insights into suitable allocations.

10. Review and Reevaluate:

- Continuously review your asset allocation strategy and reevaluate it in light of changing circumstances. Regular assessments ensure that your investments remain in harmony with your financial journey.

Just as navigators rely on their navigational charts, you can use asset allocation strategies as your investment compass. By aligning your allocation with your age, risk tolerance, and financial goals, you create a well-tailored portfolio that optimizes returns while managing risk. So, set sail with the power of asset allocation, and let your well-calibrated investment strategy guide you towards financial prosperity on this extraordinary voyage of wealth-building.

Tax-Efficient Investing and Retirement Accounts (401(k), IRA, etc.)

As skillful navigators optimize their resources, you too can employ tax-efficient investing strategies and leverage retirement accounts to maximize your financial gains. Now, we'll explore how these tools can steer you towards greater wealth while minimizing your tax burden:

1. Tax-Efficient Investing:

- Tax-efficient investing aims to minimize the impact of taxes on your investment returns. Strategies may include holding tax-efficient assets, taking advantage of tax-loss harvesting, and being mindful of tax implications when rebalancing your portfolio.

2. Utilize Retirement Accounts:

- Contribute to retirement accounts, such as 401(k)s and Individual Retirement Accounts (IRAs), to benefit from their tax advantages. These accounts offer tax deferral or tax-free growth, allowing your investments to compound more efficiently.

3. Traditional 401(k) and IRA:

- Contributions to traditional retirement accounts are made with pre-tax dollars, reducing your taxable income for the year you contribute. Taxes on earnings are deferred until withdrawals are made in retirement.

4. Roth 401(k) and IRA:

- Roth retirement accounts are funded with after-tax dollars, meaning you don't get an immediate tax deduction. However, qualified withdrawals in retirement are tax-free, providing tax-free growth potential.

5. Employer Matching Contributions:

- Take full advantage of employer matching contributions to your retirement accounts. Employer matches are essentially free money that boosts your retirement savings.

6. Maximize Contributions:

- Contribute the maximum allowed amount to your retirement accounts whenever possible. Doing so helps you build a substantial retirement nest egg and takes full advantage of their tax benefits.

7. Tax-Advantaged Investments:

- Consider investing in tax-advantaged vehicles like municipal bonds or tax-free mutual funds, which generate income that may be exempt from federal or state taxes.

8. Asset Location Strategy:

- Strategically place assets in different account types to optimize tax efficiency. For example, holding tax-inefficient assets in tax-advantaged accounts can reduce tax liability.

9. Required Minimum Distributions (RMDs):

- Be aware of RMD rules for traditional retirement accounts. Once you reach the required age, you must withdraw a minimum amount annually, subject to taxation.

10. Seek Professional Guidance:

- Tax planning can be complex, especially when it comes to retirement accounts and investment strategies. Consult with a tax advisor or financial professional to create a tax-efficient plan tailored to your situation.

By incorporating tax-efficient investing strategies and maximizing the benefits of retirement accounts, you can chart a course towards a financially rewarding future. Like savvy navigators avoiding obstacles, you'll navigate the tax landscape wisely, ensuring that your hard-earned wealth is preserved and optimized. So, set sail with tax efficiency as your compass, and let your prudent financial decisions guide you on this remarkable voyage of prosperity and financial security.

Chapter 7: Navigating Debt and Credit

Differentiating Between Good and Bad Debt

In chapter 7, we will explore the intricacies of debt and credit, much like navigators maneuvering through treacherous waters. By understanding the distinction between good and bad debt, you can chart a course towards financial freedom and avoid potential pitfalls along the way:

1. Defining Debt:

- Debt refers to borrowed money that must be repaid over time, typically with interest. It can be a valuable financial tool if managed wisely.

2. Good Debt:

- Good debt is an investment in your future or assets that can appreciate over time or generate income. Examples include student loans for education, mortgages for real estate, or business loans to fund a profitable venture.

3. Building Wealth:

- Good debt, when used prudently, can help you build wealth and create opportunities that may not be attainable with cash alone.

4. Consideration of Interest Rates:

- Good debt often comes with low-interest rates, making it more affordable and manageable in the long run.

5. Bad Debt:

- Bad debt is incurred for non-essential or short-term expenses that do not provide lasting value. Examples include high-interest credit card debt for unnecessary purchases or loans to finance extravagant vacations.

6. Draining Financial Resources:

- Bad debt can drain your financial resources, hinder wealth-building efforts, and create a cycle of financial stress.

7. Impact on Credit Score:

- Good debt managed responsibly can positively impact your credit score, making it easier to obtain credit and secure better interest rates in the future.

8. Impact on Financial Health:

- Bad debt can negatively affect your financial health, leading to missed payments, increased interest charges, and potential damage to your credit score.

9. Repayment Strategies:

- When dealing with debt, focus on developing a repayment strategy that targets high-interest or bad debt first, while maintaining payments on good debt to continue building assets.

10. Avoiding Unnecessary Debt:

- Navigators carefully assess the necessity of their cargo before embarking on a voyage. Similarly, evaluate the need and long-term value of each potential debt before taking it on.

By discerning between good and bad debt, you can navigate the waters of credit responsibly, avoiding turbulent financial storms. Understanding the potential benefits and drawbacks of debt empowers you to make informed financial decisions and steer your course towards a brighter financial future. So, set sail with financial prudence as your guide, and let your journey towards financial freedom be characterized by sound debt management and credit responsibility.

Strategies for Managing and Reducing High-Interest Debts

Just as skillful navigators chart the most efficient routes, you too can navigate the path to financial freedom by managing and reducing high-interest debts. Effective strategies to help you steer clear of debt storms and reach calmer financial waters:

1. Create a Debt Repayment Plan:

- List all your high-interest debts, including credit card balances and personal loans. Develop a structured repayment plan, focusing on the most burdensome debts first.

2. Pay More than the Minimum:

- Whenever possible, pay more than the minimum amount due on your high-interest debts. By doing so, you'll accelerate your progress and reduce interest costs.

3. Debt Snowball Method:

- Consider using the debt snowball method, where you prioritize paying off the smallest debt first, then roll the payments into the next debt on the list. This approach provides a psychological boost as you clear each debt.

4. Debt Avalanche Method:

- Alternatively, implement the debt avalanche method, targeting debts with the highest interest rates first. This approach saves more on interest payments in the long run.

5. Consolidate Debts:

- Explore debt consolidation options, such as balance transfer credit cards or personal consolidation loans with lower interest rates. This can streamline your payments and potentially save on interest.

6. Negotiate Lower Interest Rates:

- Contact your creditors and negotiate for lower interest rates, especially if you have a good payment history. A reduced interest rate can significantly ease your debt burden.

7. Cut Unnecessary Expenses:

- Temporarily cut discretionary expenses and redirect the savings towards debt repayment. Sacrifices now can lead to a debt-free future.

8. Increase Your Income:

- Explore opportunities to increase your income, such as taking on a part-time job or freelancing. The extra earnings can be dedicated to paying off high-interest debts.

9. Avoid Taking on New Debt:

- While managing existing debts, avoid taking on new high-interest debt. Focus on breaking the cycle of borrowing and diligently pay off what you owe.

10. Seek Professional Guidance:

- If managing your debts becomes overwhelming, consider seeking help from a reputable credit counseling agency or financial advisor. They can provide guidance on debt management and financial planning.

By employing these strategies, you can navigate the waters of high-interest debts with confidence. Like a skilled captain, you'll steer your financial ship towards calmer waters, free from the burden of excessive debt. So, set sail with determination, and let your commitment to debt management lead you to a brighter and more financially secure future on this remarkable voyage to financial freedom.

Building and Maintaining a Healthy Credit Score

Just as navigators maintain their vessels to ensure smooth sailing, you too can build and maintain a healthy credit score to navigate the financial world with ease. Building strategies to help you build, improve, and sustain a strong credit score:

1. Check Your Credit Report Regularly:

- Obtain your credit report from each of the major credit bureaus (Equifax, Experian, and TransUnion) annually. Review it for inaccuracies, errors, or potential signs of identity theft.

2. Establish Credit History:

- If you're new to credit, consider starting with a secured credit card or becoming an authorized user on someone else's credit card. Timely payments on these accounts will help you build a positive credit history.

3. Pay Bills on Time:

- Timely payment of bills, including credit cards, loans, and utility bills, is crucial for a healthy credit score. Late payments can have a significant negative impact.

4. Keep Credit Utilization Low:

- Aim to keep your credit card balances low in relation to your credit limits. High credit utilization can lower your credit score.

5. Diversify Your Credit Mix:

- Having a mix of different types of credit accounts, such as credit cards, installment loans, and retail accounts, can positively impact your credit score.

6. Avoid Opening Too Many New Accounts:

- Opening several new credit accounts within a short period can negatively affect your credit score. It may indicate a higher risk of borrowing.

7. Length of Credit History:

- The age of your credit accounts plays a role in determining your credit score. Keep older accounts open, even if you don't use them frequently, to demonstrate a longer credit history.

8. Use Credit Responsibly:

- Demonstrating responsible credit use over time will help boost your credit score. Avoid maxing out credit cards or carrying high balances.

9. Correct Inaccuracies Promptly:

- If you find any errors on your credit report, dispute them with the credit bureaus to have them corrected promptly.

10. Patience and Persistence:

- Building a healthy credit score takes time and discipline. Be patient, make responsible financial decisions, and your efforts will be rewarded.

By adopting these credit-building strategies, you can maintain smooth sailing in the world of credit. Like a well-maintained ship, your strong credit score will open doors to better loan terms, lower interest rates, and more financial opportunities. So, set sail with credit responsibility as your compass, and let your excellent credit score guide you towards a stable and prosperous financial voyage.

Chapter 8: Realizing Financial Freedom

Understanding the Concept of Financial Independence and Early Retirement

We'll embark on a journey to explore the liberating concept of financial independence and the possibility of early retirement. Like expert navigators who set their sights on unexplored horizons, you'll discover the principles and strategies that can lead you to a life of financial freedom:

1. Defining Financial Independence:

- Financial independence refers to a state where your passive income—income generated from investments and other sources—exceeds your living expenses. You are no longer reliant on a traditional job for financial sustenance.

2. Achieving Financial Freedom:

- Financial independence allows you to make life decisions based on your passions and values rather than financial constraints. You can choose how to spend your time, pursue meaningful endeavors, and focus on personal growth.

3. The Path to Early Retirement:

- Early retirement involves leaving the workforce and enjoying financial independence at a younger age than the traditional retirement age. It requires careful planning, disciplined saving, and strategic investing.

4. Creating Multiple Income Streams:

- To achieve financial independence, consider diversifying your income streams beyond your primary job. Explore investment income, side businesses, or passive income sources.

5. Setting Achievable Financial Goals:

- Define your financial goals, both short-term and long-term. Establish a clear plan to reach them, including the amount you need to achieve financial independence.

6. Embracing Frugality and Minimalism:

- Embrace a frugal lifestyle to maximize your savings and reduce unnecessary expenses. Adopting minimalism can help you focus on what truly brings you happiness and fulfillment.

7. Implementing the 4% Rule:

- The 4% rule is a widely used guideline for early retirement planning. It suggests that if you withdraw 4% of your portfolio's value annually, adjusted for inflation, your funds should last 30 years or more.

8. Staying Flexible and Adaptable:

- Early retirement plans may require adjustments along the way. Remain flexible and adaptable to changes in financial markets and personal circumstances.

9. Seeking Professional Advice:

- Early retirement planning can be complex. Consult with a financial advisor to help you create a customized plan that aligns with your specific goals and risk tolerance.

10. Fostering Financial Literacy:

- Like skilled navigators who study charts and maps, dedicate time to improve your financial literacy. Knowledge is a powerful tool in your journey to financial freedom.

By understanding the principles of financial independence and early retirement, you can set a course towards a life of choice and abundance. Much like navigating uncharted waters, achieving financial freedom requires diligence, resourcefulness, and the willingness to embrace new opportunities. So, set sail with the vision of financial independence, and let your journey towards early retirement be guided by purpose, passion, and the pursuit of a truly fulfilling life.

The Role of Passive Income Streams in Achieving Financial Freedom

Just as skilled navigators utilize favorable winds to propel their ships, you too can harness the power of passive income streams to accelerate your journey towards financial freedom. Passive income in building sustainable wealth and achieving financial independence:

1. Defining Passive Income:

- Passive income refers to money earned with little active effort or direct involvement. It is generated from assets or investments that work for you, rather than you working for them.

2. Diversifying Income Sources:

- Relying solely on earned income from a job may limit your ability to achieve financial freedom. Diversifying with passive income sources provides financial stability and resilience.

3. Creating Financial Resilience:

- Passive income streams act as a safety net during economic downturns or unexpected life events. They can help you maintain financial stability even when your primary job is affected.

4. Building Wealth:

- Passive income streams allow you to accumulate wealth over time without trading your time for money. Investments in real estate, dividend-paying stocks, or businesses can grow your net worth.

5. Reducing Reliance on Traditional Employment:

- As passive income grows, you may have the option to work less or retire early, moving closer to the goal of financial freedom.

6. Different Types of Passive Income:

- Passive income can be earned from rental properties, dividends, interest from savings accounts or bonds, peer-to-peer lending, royalties from creative works, and income from online businesses.

7. Investing for Passive Income:

- Strategic investments that generate consistent cash flow are key to creating sustainable passive income. Consider income-producing assets that align with your risk tolerance and financial goals.

8. The Snowball Effect:

- As passive income streams increase, you can reinvest the earnings to acquire additional income-producing assets, accelerating the growth of your passive income over time.

9. Time Freedom:

- Passive income allows you to have more control over your time. It grants the freedom to pursue passions, spend time with loved ones, or engage in philanthropic endeavors.

10. Be Patient and Persistent:

- Building passive income streams requires patience and persistence. It may take time to establish, but the long-term benefits are worth the effort.

By incorporating passive income streams into your financial strategy, you can chart a course towards greater financial independence. Like a skilled captain navigating with a favorable current, you'll sail confidently towards a life where your money works for you, providing the freedom and flexibility to pursue your dreams. So, set sail with passive income as your guiding star, and let the power of passive wealth-building lead you on this extraordinary voyage to financial freedom.

Creating a Sustainable Withdrawal Plan for Retirement

Just as navigators plan their routes to conserve resources and reach their destinations, you too can create a sustainable withdrawal plan for retirement to ensure your financial security throughout your golden years. Essential strategies for managing your retirement savings and generating a consistent income stream:

1. Assessing Your Retirement Needs:

- Start by estimating your expected retirement expenses, considering factors such as housing, healthcare, travel, and lifestyle choices. Understanding your needs will guide your withdrawal plan.

2. The 4% Rule Revisited:

- Revisit the 4% rule, which suggests withdrawing 4% of your initial retirement portfolio balance annually, adjusted for inflation. This rule can serve as a baseline for setting your withdrawal rate.

3. Account for Inflation:

- Factor inflation into your withdrawal plan to ensure that your income retains its purchasing power over time.

4. Tax-Efficient Withdrawals:

- Plan your withdrawals strategically to minimize tax liabilities. Consider withdrawing from different account types (e.g., taxable, tax-deferred, and tax-free) to optimize tax efficiency.

5. Using Required Minimum Distributions (RMDs):

- If you have traditional retirement accounts, be aware of RMD rules, which require minimum withdrawals starting at age 72 (or earlier if you turned 70½ before January 1, 2020). Account for RMDs in your plan.

6. Dynamic Withdrawal Strategies:

- Implement a dynamic withdrawal approach that adjusts your annual withdrawals based on market conditions and portfolio performance. This strategy can help preserve your savings during market downturns.

7. Stay Flexible:

- Be prepared to adjust your withdrawal plan as life circumstances change. Stay flexible to accommodate unexpected expenses or fluctuations in your financial situation.

8. Preserve Capital for Growth:

- Balance the need for income with the desire to preserve your capital for long-term growth. Overly conservative withdrawal rates may hinder your portfolio's ability to keep up with inflation.

9. Consider Annuities or Longevity Insurance:

- Annuities or longevity insurance can provide guaranteed income for life, offering additional security against outliving your savings.

10. Consult a Financial Advisor:

- Retirement planning can be complex. Consult with a financial advisor to develop a personalized withdrawal strategy tailored to your unique situation and goals.

By crafting a sustainable withdrawal plan, you can navigate the seas of retirement with confidence, enjoying financial security and peace of mind. Like an expert navigator charting a steady course, your thoughtful withdrawal strategy will help you preserve your wealth, maintain a consistent income, and embrace the fulfilling lifestyle you envision for your retirement years. So, set sail with prudence and foresight, and let your sustainable withdrawal plan guide you on this remarkable voyage of retirement fulfillment and financial stability.

Chapter 9: Safeguarding Your Financial Future

The Importance of Insurance in Protecting Your Wealth and Assets

We'll explore the crucial role of insurance in safeguarding your financial well-being, much like skilled navigators prepare for potential storms to protect their vessels. Insurance serves as a vital tool in securing your wealth and assets against unforeseen risks:

1. Understanding Risk Exposure:

- Begin by assessing your risk exposure—potential threats that could lead to financial losses. These risks may include health issues, accidents, property damage, liability claims, or even premature death.

2. Health Insurance:

- Health insurance protects you from the high costs of medical treatments, hospitalization, and prescription drugs. It provides peace of mind, knowing that you and your loved ones can access necessary healthcare without significant financial strain.

3. Property Insurance:

- Property insurance, such as homeowner's insurance or renter's insurance, shields your home and belongings from damage or theft. It ensures you can rebuild or replace your property in case of an unfortunate event.

4. Auto Insurance:

- Auto insurance is essential for protecting yourself and others from financial liabilities arising from accidents. It covers damages to vehicles, medical expenses, and legal costs associated with accidents.

5. Life Insurance:

- Life insurance provides financial protection for your loved ones in the event of your passing. It can cover funeral expenses, pay off debts, replace lost income, and help secure your family's future.

6. Disability Insurance:

- Disability insurance safeguards your income if you become unable to work due to a disability. It helps you maintain your financial stability during challenging times.

7. Liability Insurance:

- Liability insurance shields you from financial liabilities resulting from accidental injuries or property damage to others. This coverage is crucial to protect your wealth from potential lawsuits.

8. Long-Term Care Insurance:

- Long-term care insurance helps cover the costs of assisted living or nursing home care, protecting your assets and savings from being depleted by long-term care expenses.

9. Business Insurance:

- If you own a business, consider business insurance to protect your enterprise from unexpected events, lawsuits, property damage, and liability claims.

10. Regular Policy Review:

- Regularly review your insurance coverage to ensure it aligns with your current needs and life circumstances. Adjust coverage as necessary to maintain adequate protection.

By incorporating insurance into your financial plan, you fortify your financial vessel against potential storms. Like expert navigators who prepare for any eventuality, securing comprehensive insurance coverage ensures you and your loved ones are shielded from the financial impact of unexpected events. So, set sail with confidence, knowing that your prudent insurance choices safeguard your wealth and assets, guiding you towards a more secure and prosperous financial future.

Estate Planning Essentials, Including Wills and Trusts

Just as navigators chart their course with precision, estate planning allows you to carefully design the distribution of your wealth and assets, leaving a legacy for your loved ones. Now, we'll explore the critical elements of estate planning, including wills and trusts, to ensure your financial journey extends beyond your lifetime:

1. Estate Planning Goals:

- Begin by defining your estate planning goals. Consider how you want your assets to be distributed, who will handle your affairs if you become incapacitated, and how you want to support your loved ones.

2. Writing a Will:

- A will is a fundamental document that outlines how your assets will be distributed after your death. It allows you to appoint an executor to carry out your wishes and name guardians for minor children.

3. Updating Your Will Regularly:

- Life circumstances change, so regularly update your will to reflect new beneficiaries, assets, or changes in your preferences.

4. Consider a Living Trust:

- A living trust allows you to transfer assets to a trust during your lifetime. It provides flexibility, privacy, and can help your loved ones avoid probate court proceedings.

5. Designating Beneficiaries:

- Review and designate beneficiaries for retirement accounts, life insurance policies, and other accounts. These designations often supersede what is written in your will.

6. Appointing a Power of Attorney:

- Appoint a durable power of attorney to manage your financial affairs if you become incapacitated and are unable to make decisions yourself.

7. Healthcare Directives:

- Prepare healthcare directives, including a living will and a healthcare proxy. These documents ensure your healthcare preferences are followed if you are unable to communicate.

8. Minimizing Estate Taxes:

- Consult with a financial advisor or estate planning attorney to explore strategies to minimize estate taxes, allowing more of your wealth to pass to your beneficiaries.

9. Trusts for Minor Children:

- Establish trusts to manage assets for minor children until they reach a certain age or milestone. This ensures that the assets are used for their benefit responsibly.

10. Seek Professional Guidance:

- Estate planning can be complex, so seek advice from an experienced estate planning attorney who can help create a comprehensive plan tailored to your specific wishes and needs.

By embracing estate planning essentials, you ensure that your financial legacy carries forward, benefiting your loved ones and securing your wealth's continuity. Like skilled navigators preparing for a smooth transition of command, estate planning empowers you to dictate your financial journey's direction, providing lasting peace of mind for you and your family. So, set sail with the knowledge that your estate plan will guide your wealth's passage, leaving behind a legacy that endures through generations.

Long-Term Care Planning and Retirement Healthcare Considerations

Just as expert navigators prepare for extended voyages, long-term care planning and retirement healthcare considerations are vital for a smooth and secure retirement journey. The importance of preparing for potential healthcare needs in your golden years:

1. Understanding Long-Term Care (LTC) Needs:

- Long-term care refers to the assistance required for individuals with chronic medical conditions or disabilities. It includes services like nursing home care, assisted living, and home healthcare.

2. Assessing Your Long-Term Care Insurance Options:

- Consider long-term care insurance as a way to protect your assets from the high costs of extended care services. Explore different policies and assess which one best meets your needs.

3. Evaluating Medicare Coverage:

- Understand what Medicare covers and what it does not when it comes to long-term care services. Consider supplemental insurance plans to fill any gaps in coverage.

4. Retirement Healthcare Expenses:

- Budget for healthcare expenses in retirement, including Medicare premiums, deductibles, and potential out-of-pocket costs for medical services.

5. Health Savings Accounts (HSAs):

- Maximize contributions to HSAs if you're eligible. HSAs offer tax advantages and can be used to pay for qualified medical expenses in retirement.

6. Consider Longevity and Health Factors:

- Factor in your family's longevity and any potential health issues when planning for retirement healthcare needs. Prepare for the possibility of extended care requirements.

7. Explore Retirement Communities and Facilities:

- Research retirement communities and facilities that offer various levels of care, from independent living to skilled nursing. Evaluate their services, costs, and reputations.

8. Make Healthy Lifestyle Choices:

- Prioritize your health and wellness to reduce the risk of chronic conditions and enhance your quality of life in retirement.

9. Incorporate End-of-Life Planning:

- Discuss end-of-life wishes with your loved ones and create an advance healthcare directive to ensure your preferences are respected during medical decision-making.

10. Regularly Review and Adjust Plans:

- Healthcare needs can change over time, so regularly review and adjust your long-term care and retirement healthcare plans as necessary.

By including long-term care planning and retirement healthcare considerations in your financial strategy, you set a steady course towards a secure and comfortable retirement journey. Like a navigator planning for all contingencies, preparing for potential healthcare needs ensures you'll enjoy a fulfilling retirement with peace of mind, knowing that your healthcare needs are taken care of. So, set sail with prudence and foresight, and let your comprehensive retirement healthcare plan guide you towards a life of health and happiness in your well-deserved retirement years.

Chapter 10: Mastering the Financial Mindset

Overcoming Common Money Mindset Blocks and Limiting Beliefs

The significance of cultivating a positive financial mindset, much like skilled navigators maintain a clear and focused mental compass. Overcoming money mindset blocks and limiting beliefs is essential for achieving lasting financial success and well-being:

1. Identifying Money Mindset Blocks:

- Begin by recognizing any negative beliefs or attitudes you hold about money. Common mindset blocks may include fear of scarcity, self-doubt regarding financial abilities, or a belief that wealth is unattainable.

2. Shifting from Scarcity to Abundance:

- Transform a scarcity mindset into an abundance mindset. Instead of dwelling on what you lack, focus on the opportunities and resources available to you.

3. Acknowledging the Influence of Childhood Experiences:

- Reflect on how your upbringing and early experiences with money have shaped your beliefs. Identify any limiting beliefs rooted in past experiences and challenge their validity.

4. Embracing a Growth Mindset:

- Cultivate a growth mindset, believing that your financial knowledge and abilities can improve with effort and dedication. See setbacks as learning opportunities and embrace a lifelong journey of financial learning.

5. Building Confidence in Financial Decision-Making:

- Strengthen your confidence in handling financial matters. Seek education, read financial literature, and make small, informed decisions to build competence over time.

6. Avoiding Comparison Trap:

- Resist comparing your financial situation to others. Everyone's journey is unique, and external comparisons can lead to dissatisfaction and misguided decisions.

7. Rewriting Limiting Money Stories:

- Challenge and rewrite any negative money stories you've told yourself. Replace them with empowering narratives that align with your financial goals.

8. Visualization and Affirmations:

- Use visualization and affirmations to reinforce positive financial beliefs. Envision yourself achieving financial success and repeat affirmations that support your financial goals.

9. Surrounding Yourself with Positive Influences:

- Surround yourself with individuals who have a positive and empowering financial mindset. Seek support from like-minded peers or mentors who can inspire and encourage you.

10. Practicing Gratitude and Contentment:

- Develop gratitude for what you have and cultivate contentment in the present moment. Recognize that financial success is not solely defined by material wealth.

By mastering the financial mindset, you set sail with an unwavering sense of purpose and determination. Just as skilled navigators use their mental acuity to navigate uncharted waters, cultivating a positive financial mindset allows you to steer your financial journey with confidence and clarity. So, set sail with an empowered financial mindset, and let your positive beliefs and attitudes guide you towards a life of financial abundance and fulfillment.

Cultivating a Positive and Abundant Money Mindset

Much like expert navigators who stay focused on their destination, cultivating a positive and abundant money mindset is the compass that guides you towards financial prosperity. We'll explore essential strategies to nurture a mindset that attracts abundance and empowers your financial journey:

1. Gratitude Practice:

- Start each day with a gratitude practice. Acknowledge and appreciate the financial blessings you have, no matter how big or small.

2. Focus on Possibilities:

- Shift your focus from limitations to possibilities. Train your mind to see opportunities for growth and improvement in every financial situation.

3. Affirmations and Visualization:

- Use positive affirmations and visualization techniques to reinforce your belief in financial abundance. Imagine yourself achieving your financial goals with clarity and detail.

4. Embrace Financial Education:

- Pursue ongoing financial education to build confidence and competence. Knowledge empowers you to make informed decisions and take control of your financial journey.

5. Learn from Setbacks:

- Instead of seeing setbacks as failures, view them as learning experiences. Embrace the lessons they offer and use them as stepping stones to future success.

6. Surround Yourself with Positivity:

- Surround yourself with positive influences—people who uplift and encourage your financial aspirations. Limit exposure to negativity or pessimism.

7. Focus on Solutions, Not Problems:

- When facing financial challenges, focus on finding solutions rather than dwelling on the problems. Approach difficulties with a problem-solving mindset.

8. Celebrate Financial Wins:

- Celebrate every financial accomplishment, no matter how small. Acknowledging your progress boosts your confidence and motivates further success.

9. Practice Mindfulness:

- Stay present and mindful of your financial decisions. Avoid making impulsive choices and consider the long-term impact of your actions.

10. Release Money Guilt and Shame:

- Let go of any guilt or shame associated with money. Accept that everyone makes financial mistakes, and those mistakes don't define your worth or potential.

By cultivating a positive and abundant money mindset, you harness the winds of possibility and navigate your financial journey with purpose and optimism. Like a skilled navigator steering a ship through calm and stormy seas, your mindset will shape your financial decisions and outcomes. So, set sail with a mindset of abundance and prosperity, and let your positive beliefs guide you towards a life of financial fulfillment and empowerment.

- The connection between financial health and overall well-being

Did you love *The Financial Bullet Blueprint*? Then you should read *Financial Freedom Roadmap - Achieving Early Retirement through the FIRE Movement*[1] by Alex Thompson!

[2]

Are you longing to break free from the shackles of financial stress and achieve early retirement? Look no further! "Financial Freedom Roadmap: Achieving Early Retirement through the FIRE Movement" is your definitive guide to unlocking the doors to financial independence and retiring on your terms.

In this enlightening book, you'll embark on a transformative journey that will revolutionize your relationship with money. Drawing inspiration from the popular FIRE (Financial Independence, Retire Early) movement, this comprehensive guide offers practical advice,

1. https://books2read.com/u/m2q8W1

2. https://books2read.com/u/m2q8W1

proven strategies, and invaluable insights to help you chart your path towards financial freedom.

The journey begins with a deep dive into the FIRE mindset. In Chapter 1, you'll unravel the core principles and mindset shifts that fuel the FIRE movement. Learn how to reframe your thinking, prioritize your values, and align your actions with your long-term financial goals.

Armed with this powerful mindset, you'll navigate Chapter 2, where you'll gain mastery over personal finance. From budgeting and debt management to establishing emergency funds and building a strong financial foundation, you'll acquire the tools and knowledge to take full control of your financial destiny.

Next, in Chapter 3, you'll uncover the art of maximizing income generation. Whether it's leveraging your career, creating lucrative side hustles, or exploring passive income streams, you'll discover proven strategies to boost your earning potential and fast-track your journey to financial independence.

Chapter 4 will guide you through the realm of minimizing expenses and lifestyle optimization. Discover practical techniques to trim unnecessary costs, adopt a frugal mindset, and design a fulfilling life that aligns with your financial goals. Learn how to optimize every aspect of your lifestyle to free up resources for wealth accumulation.

As your financial confidence soars, you'll venture into Chapter 5, where you'll craft a robust investment strategy tailored to your FIRE aspirations. Gain insights into asset allocation, diversification, and the power of compounding to build a resilient investment portfolio that propels you towards early retirement.

Finally, in Chapter 6, you'll unlock the secrets of tax optimization and retirement accounts. Unravel strategies to maximize tax advantages, leverage retirement accounts such as IRAs and 401(k)s, and supercharge your wealth accumulation while minimizing tax burdens.

"Financial Freedom Roadmap: Achieving Early Retirement through the FIRE Movement" is your ultimate companion on the quest for financial independence. Bursting with practical advice, real-life examples, and step-by-step instructions, this book empowers you to take charge of your financial future. Whether you're just starting your journey or seeking to refine your strategies, this comprehensive roadmap will guide you towards the life of freedom and abundance you desire. Begin your journey today and set yourself on the path to early retirement and financial fulfillment!

Also by Alex Thompson

Alex on Finance

Financial Freedom Roadmap - Achieving Early Retirement through the FIRE Movement

The Art of Strategic Innovation

Beyond Cash - The Evolution of Digital Payment Systems and the Future of Money

Preserving Wealth in Inflationary Times - Strategies for Protecting Your Financial Future

Standalone

Side Hustle Success: Unlocking Your Entrepreneurial Potential

Side Hustle Success: The Ultimate Guide to Passive and Financial Freedom

Mastering the Markets: Advanced Trading Strategies for Success and Ethical Trading Practices

Financial Fortitude

Mastering the Art of Upselling

The Financial Bullet Blueprint

www.ingramcontent.com/pod-product-compliance
Lightning Source LLC
LaVergne TN
LVHW090427210926
848480LV00002B/719